THIS BOOK BELONGS TO

_____

13-Digit ISBN: 978-1-60433-817-1
10-Digit ISBN: 1-60433-817-2

This book may be ordered by mail from the publisher. Please include $5.99 for postage and handling. Please support your local bookseller first!
Books published by Cider Mill Press Book Publishers are available at special discounts for bulk purchases in the United States by corporations, institutions, and other organizations. For more information, please contact the publisher.
Cider Mill Press Book Publishers
"Where Good Books Are Ready for Press"
PO Box 454
12 Spring Street
Kennebunkport, Maine 04046
Visit us online!
cidermillpress.com

Typography: Chevalier Stripes, Georgia, Hoefler Text, and Voluta Script Pro
Image Credits:
Front endpapers: Edgar Allan Poe House, Philadelphia, Pennsylvania. Poe's time in Pennsylvania was the most productive of his career, during which he wrote some of his most famous short stories. Photo courtesy of the Library of Congress. Portrait of Edgar Allan Poe painted by Samuel Stillman Osgood, original in the possession of the New York Historical Society. Photo courtesy of Wikimedia Commons
Back endpapers: Photo of a daguerreotype of Edgar Allan Poe by W.S. Hartshorn, 1849. Photo courtesy of the Library of Congress
Poe Cottage, Fordham, New York. The Poe family's final home before the deaths of Virginia and Edgar Allan Poe. Engraved by Benjamin F. Buck and courtesy of the Library of Congress.
Courtesy of the Library of Congress: ix, Edgar Allan Poe and Richard Gimbel; 46-47, Fred C. Berte; 75, Mrs. Norman Burwell and Archer G. Jones; 88, Arthur E. Becher; 95; Courtesy of Shutterstock: Front o-band, 20, 61, 156, 185, Everett Historical; 34-35, 169, Guillermo Olaizola; Courtesy of Wikimedia Commons: 110, Thomas B. Welch and Adam B. Waler; 133, Midnightdreary; 141, Midnightdreary/Edgar Allan Poe.

Printed in China
1 2 3 4 5 6 7 8 9 0
First Edition

EDGAR ALLAN POE

SIGNATURE NOTEBOOK

CIDER MILL
PRESS

BOOK
PUBLISHERS

KENNEBUNKPORT, MAINE

Introduction

J. Gerald Kennedy
Author of *Poe, Death, and the Life of Writing*
and *Strange Nation: Literary Nationalism and
Cultural Conflict in the Age of Poe*, and editor
of *The Portable Edgar Allan Poe*.

*T*hough Poe lived two centuries ago, his writings still grip readers today. His darker themes—death, madness, perverseness, and violence—anticipated the horrors of twentieth-century history and our millennial Age of Terror.

Born in 1809, Poe inhabited a nation still seeking an identity. Orphaned at two, he sailed with his foster parents, the Allans, to England in 1815 and attended boarding schools near London. There, he read by candlelight and wrote with a quill pen. He grew to love literature, poring over story books and recitation textbooks. Like other schoolboys, Poe probably read Coleridge and Byron, perhaps memorizing lines of verse. Before leaving England in 1820, he vowed to become a poet.

Indeed, he returned to America with a sheaf of poems, and his Richmond school years inspired new verse as well as poetical craft. After a stressful year at the University of Virginia in 1826, Poe rebuked miserly John Allan, left home, and published a slim book of poetry called *Tamerlane* in Boston. Two subsequent volumes showed talent but furnished no livelihood.

In Baltimore, Poe then began writing magazine tales. His first stories appeared in 1832, and he later found employment at the *Southern Literary Messenger* in Richmond. As a "magazinist," he composed reviews, articles, and notes. But Poe could not find a publisher willing to collect his "mystical" tales into one volume. Instead, he was told to write a novel. Poe faced a crushing workload supporting his cousin-wife, Virginia, and her mother. Unsteadiness and indignation finally cost him his job. Moving to New York, Poe remained unemployed as the Panic of 1837 brought destitution and delayed his novel.

When *The Narrative of Arthur Gordon Pym* appeared in 1838, Poe was living in Philadelphia. His hoax described a fantastic voyage to the South Seas but sold poorly. Yet editorial stints with *Burton's Gentleman's Magazine* and *Graham's*

Magazine increased Poe's notoriety as a critic and let him showcase brilliant tales. His twenty-five *Tales of the Grotesque and Arabesque* appeared in 1840, and his prize-winning story, "The Gold-Bug," brought acclaim in 1843. But the worsening of Virginia's tuberculosis alarmed him, and he returned to New York in 1844, seeking steady work and healthier surroundings. That year, Poe claimed that "a mania for composition" sometimes caused him to "scribble all day, and read all night."

Poe published his most famous poem, "The Raven," in 1845 and joined the staff of *The Broadway Journal.* He also entered salon culture as a literary celebrity. But the newspaper's demise and his wife's death one year later marked the beginning of Poe's decline. He tried to rebound from adversity in 1848 with a baffling treatise titled *Eureka*, while his romantic gambits grew increasingly bewildering. When a journey south reunited him with his childhood sweetheart, now a wealthy widow, he seemed on the verge of a happy remarriage. But in October, 1849, he succumbed to drink and died in Baltimore.

Poe pursued the life of writing. His penmanship could be graceful, and he labored to produce impeccable manuscripts. Sometimes he pasted handwritten pages together, creating scrolls. He became obsessed with graphology, introducing a magazine feature called "Autography" that analyzed a writer's character from the signature and handwriting. Proposing a monthly magazine of his own, he called it *The Penn* and later *The Stylus*, branding his journal with the image of a hand holding a pen.

Though fascinated by machines, Poe enjoyed the intimacy of handwriting and would have resisted modern keyboards. He experimented in different styles and genres. He was also preoccupied with "secret writing": using cryptography to encode messages. Poe built "The Gold-Bug" around a coded message inscribed in invisible ink, and he sometimes used similar tricks in his poems. His detective story, "The Purloined Letter," famously concerns writing and power.

But Poe also protested composition drudgery. In 1844, he satirized "Thingum Bob" as a veritable writing machine. The following year, in "Some Secrets of the Magazine Prison-House," he advocated for literary copyright by revealing how publishers stole the writing of unpaid "poor devil authors." He became fascinated with "anastatic printing," an experimental method of reproducing a written

Facsimile of Edgar Allan Poe's The Raven *manuscript, exhibited at Yale University Library in honor of Poe's 150th birthday. Courtesy of Richard Gimbel.*

The Raven.

Once, upon a midnight dreary, while I pondered, weak and weary,
Over many a quaint and curious volume of forgotten lore —
While I nodded, nearly napping, suddenly there came a tapping,
As of some one gently rapping, rapping at my chamber door.
"'Tis some visiter," I muttered, "tapping at my chamber door —
           Only this and nothing more."

Ah, distinctly I remember it was in the bleak December,
And each separate dying ember wrought its ghost upon the floor.
Eagerly I wished the morrow;— vainly I had sought to borrow
From my books surcease of sorrow — sorrow for the lost Lenore —
For the rare and radiant maiden whom the angels name Lenore —
           Nameless here for evermore.

And the silken, sad, uncertain rustling of each purple curtain
Thrilled me, filled me with fantastic terrors never felt before;
So that now, to still the beating of my heart, I stood repeating
"'Tis some visiter entreating entrance at my chamber door —
Some late visiter entreating entrance at my chamber door;—
           This it is and nothing more."

Presently my soul grew stronger. Hesitating then, no longer,
"Sir," said I, or Madam, truly your forgiveness I implore;
But the fact is I was napping, and so gently you came rapping,
And so faintly you came tapping, tapping at my chamber door
That I scarce was sure I heard you" — here I opened wide the door;—
           Darkness there and nothing more.

Deep into that darkness peering, long I stood there, wondering, fearing,
Doubting, dreaming dreams no mortal ever dared to dream before;
But the silence was unbroken, and the stillness gave no token,
And the only word there spoken was the whispered word, "Lenore?"
This I whispered, and an echo murmured back the word "Lenore!"
           Merely this and nothing more.

text. Poe thought this process would revolutionize publishing by eliminating typesetting and allowing authors to sell their own works. The technology depended on neat handwriting, which Poe believed would encourage "precision of thought, and luminous arrangement of matter." He grasped the dynamic relationship between writing and thought.

In "MS Found in a Bottle," Poe portrays a narrator on a doomed ship who decides to keep a record of his adventures, sealing his pages in a bottle "at the last moment." Then he absentmindedly daubs tar on a sail, which unfurls to reveal the word "DISCOVERY." The narrator takes this as a sign of his theme as a writer, hinting that, in this early tale, Poe was already seeing his own writing as an exercise in discovery.

I do not believe that any thought,
properly so called, is out of

THE REACH
OF LANGUAGE.

—*"Marginalia"* (1846)

Being everything which
now thou art,

BE NOTHING
WHICH THOU
ART NOT.

—"TO F——s S. O——d," in The Raven and Other Poems (1845)

Edgar Allan Poe (circa 1840s)

I need scarcely observe that
a poem deserves its title only
inasmuch as it excites, by

ELEVATING
THE SOUL

—"The Poetic Principle" (1850)

The garden of the Poe Museum in Richmond, Virginia

They who dream by day are cognizant of many things which

ESCAPE

those who dream only by night.

—*"Eleonora"* (1842)

And, through all, I—wrote.
THROUGH JOY AND
THROUGH SORROW,
I—WROTE....
Through sunshine and through
moonshine, I—wrote.

—The Literary Life of Thingum Bob, Esq. (December 1844)

*The Poe Cottage at Fordham, New York, Poe's final
home before his death* (circa 1900)

Depend upon it, after all, Thomas,

LITERATURE IS THE MOST NOBLE OF PROFESSIONS.

In fact, it is about the only one fit for a man. For my own part, there is no seducing me from the path.

—*Letter to Frederick W. Thomas* (February 14, 1849)

That pleasure which is at once the most pure, the most elevating, and the most intense, is derived, I maintain, from the

CONTEMPLATION OF THE BEAUTIFUL.

—*"The Philosophy of Composition"* (1846)

A depiction of Edgar Allan Poe's "The Raven," in which the poem's narrator envisions angels surrounding his dear departed Lenore. Illustrated by Gustave Dore (1883)

For my own part, I have never
had a thought which I could not

SET DOWN
IN WORDS,

with even more distinctness than
that with which I conceived it.

—*"Marginalia"* (1846)

Believe nothing you

HEAR,

and only one

HALF

that you see.

—*"The System of Doctor Tarr and Professor Fether"* (1845)

Painting of Edgar Allan Poe by Mrs. Norman Burwell (1921)

BEAUTY

is the sole legitimate province of the poem.

—*"The Philosophy of Composition"* (1846)

The grave of Edgar Allan Poe in the Westminster Burying Grounds, Baltimore, Maryland

To observe attentively is to

REMEMBER DISTINCTLY.

—*"The Murders in the Rue Morgue"* (1841)

Illustration of Edgar Allan Poe's
"The Mystery of Marie Roget" (1855)

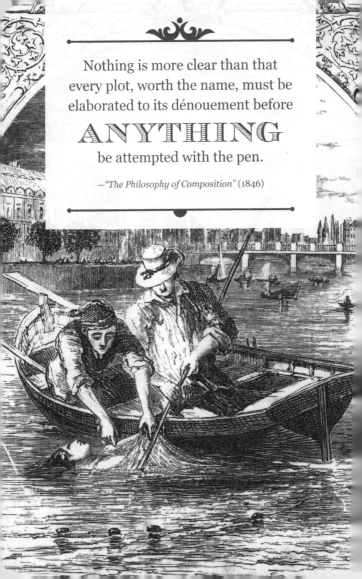

Nothing is more clear than that every plot, worth the name, must be elaborated to its dénouement before

ANYTHING

be attempted with the pen.

—*"The Philosophy of Composition"* (1846)

Music, when combined with
a pleasurable idea, is

POETRY;

music, without the idea,
is simply music; the idea,
without the music, is prose
from its very definitiveness.

—*"Letter to B—"* (1836)

THE

STYLUS

A

Monthly Journal of Literature Proper *the Fine Arts* *and the* Drama.

Auvus aliquanto STYLUS, ferreus aliquanto.
Paulus Jovius.

EDITED BY

EDGAR A. POE

Edgar Allan Poe's design for the cover of The Stylus,
Poe's would-be literary journal (circa 1840)

And while I thus spoke,
did there not cross your mind
some thought of the

PHYSICAL POWER OF WORDS?

Is not every word an impulse
on the air?

—*"The Power of Words"* (1845)

Watercolor of Edgar Allan Poe's wife, Virginia Eliza Clemm Poe,
as painted after her death (1847)

Most writers—poets in especial—prefer having it understood that they compose by a species of fine frenzy —AN ECSTATIC INTUITION— and would positively shudder at letting the public take a peep behind the scenes.

—*"The Philosophy of Composition"* (1846)

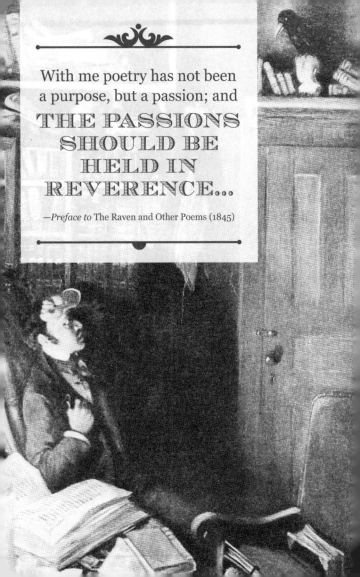

With me poetry has not been a purpose, but a passion; and **THE PASSIONS SHOULD BE HELD IN REVERENCE...**

—*Preface to* The Raven and Other Poems (1845)

An illustration of Edgar Allan Poe's "The Raven"
by Arthur E. Becher (circa 1903)

Medallion bust of Edgar Allan Poe (circa 1913)

In reading some books we occupy
ourselves chiefly with the

THOUGHTS
OF THE
AUTHOR;

in perusing others, exclusively
with our own.

—*"Marginalia"* (1844)

Ah, not in knowledge is happiness, but in the

ACQUISITION

of knowledge!

—*"The Power of Words"* (1845)

Steel engraving of Edgar Allan Poe by Thomas B. Welch
(circa 1840s)

It is impossible to say how
first the idea entered my brain;
but once conceived, it

HAUNTED ME DAY AND NIGHT.

—"The Tell-Tale Heart" (1843)

I would define, in brief,
the Poetry of words as

THE
RHYTHMICAL
CREATION OF
BEAUTY.

—*"The Poetic Principle"* (1850)